MAINE

MAINE

THE SEASONS

TERRELL S. LESTER

With essays by
Ann Beattie, Richard Ford, Richard Russo, and Elizabeth Strout

ALFRED A. KNOPF   NEW YORK   2001

Frontispiece:
Sunset from Blue Hill Overlook, Cadillac Mountain,
Acadia National Park

To my beautiful wife, Ginger, for sharing it all,

and to my mother, Doris, for planting the seed of adventure

that has led me down this road

Apple tree in snow, Deer Isle. Apple trees growing along the coast are the result of a failed agricultural industry. The apples are a favorite food of deer, and some are pressed for cider.

CONTENTS

Introduction

ix

SPRING

Essay by ELIZABETH STROUT

1

SUMMER

Essay by ANN BEATTIE

29

AUTUMN

Essay by RICHARD RUSSO

65

WINTER

Essay by RICHARD FORD

105

Acknowledgments

143

INTRODUCTION

Maine is a land of diversity and extremes. It was not created entirely by gentle and subtle forces of erosion over countless millennia, though wind and rain did play a part in shaping the granite coastline and ancient mountains. It was also gouged and scraped, ripped and polished, to its present-day topography. Forty thousand years ago, an enormous sheet of slowly migrating ice nearly two miles thick covered the land. It carried such force that it cut, ground, and shaped most of the rugged features seen here today. The land continues to be sculpted and chiseled by the relentless forces of ice, wind, and water. The Maine landscape is an ongoing geologic work of art, forever in progress, forever changing

The seasons of Maine are as diverse and extreme as its topography. I have experienced snow showers in June and have seen insects emerge from melting snow during a January thaw. The seasons rarely coincide with dates on a calendar. They are governed more by weather patterns that vary noticeably from region to region and from year to year. Spring always seems to arrive late, after a wet and muddy start. Summer days are long and filled with a warm light that starts to vanish in only a few weeks. Fall explodes in hues of red, yellow, and russet that paint every leaf, twig, forest, and field in color. Winter begins sullen and moody, with gray skies and stark landscapes. Some winter days are bright blue and crisp, others gray and subdued. At times, invading arctic weather systems transform the land into an altogether inhospitable and alien environment. Winter is by far the most enduring season in Maine, but the memory of its long, forbidding grip is lessened by the intense, if all too short, beauty of the seasons that follow.

I was a gypsy artist when I moved to the midcoast of Maine. Lured by the magnificent landscape, I wanted to experience its power and beauty, to capture its spirit as it had captured mine. I brought with me the idea that photographing the land was not simply about recording the things seen through a lens, but was more about expressing how those things made me feel. The language of camera and film are technical and specific. It is essential to understand the language of photography before you can successfully communicate through it, but it is equally essential to gain an understanding of the subject and the light that falls upon it. There is an ambience to the light in Maine that I have experienced nowhere else. It can be soft and moody one minute, then strong and dramatic the next. The environment itself is a challenge to work in. Blackflies and mosquitoes present a relentless distraction during the warmer months. Winter temperatures drop below zero on the coast, and much lower inland. There is a painful price to pay when photographing in windchill temperatures of minus fifty

Autumn storm, Schoodic Point, Acadia National Park

degrees. These elements, however, often create the most dramatic photographs. The freezing sea vapor—locals call it "sea smoke"—boils and swirls when warmer sea vapor collides with subzero air temperatures. Coastal fog masks distracting details in the background, emphasizing subjects closer at hand and turning ordinary objects into strong graphic designs. Wet, overcast autumn skies saturate colors and envelop the land with soft radiant light. I often work with a particular landscape for days or weeks to get just the right lighting conditions. I have waited years for the right conditions to photograph some subjects; still others elude me to this day.

I have heard it said that Maine is too big to explore in a lifetime, but is still small enough to try. This book is not about trying to capture all of the varied landscapes in this huge and magnificent state. Instead, I have tried to capture places that resonate with me deeply. It has not been an easy task. This is a land of tall tales and legends that are surpassed only by what you find here. It is a place to cherish, whether you spend a few days or a lifetime. It has been my privilege to work and live in such an inspirational land, and an even greater pleasure to share with you my photographic visions of this magnificent place.

TERRELL S. LESTER

Lobster-pot buoy markers, Stonington

RICHARD FORD

Winter is the season things are measured by here, the season everyone carries with them, a yearly appointment with nature when stern news could be imparted. Winter is the measure of the man (or the woman). "Are ya staying all winter, then?" they want to know, their blue eyes damp and dancing, a smile of knowing you're *not* flickering in the corners of their mouths. "Oh, you need to be here then. It's the real Maine then. Everything's *some* different. The tourists, the leaf people, they've gone back. You'd like it then." Smiling, they think I'll leave, too. "It's all shut then. It's when I like it best."

At night, a single light shines far down Linekin Bay on tiny Negro Island, where once a slave packet let off a consignment of Africans while the crew went roistering down to Portland. In the cracking cold I go down to my dock to stare off and wonder if someone's there now, just at the brink of the Atlantic. No one is, I think. It's winter. The cottages on Ocean Point, across Card Cove, are boarded, their pipes drained, rooms empty. Inside it's still. Crows are noisy, ominous in the pine thickets, their cries and wing-flaps audible in the dark. They come to the island at dusk to nest where no one is.

It's true, the roadside stands *are* shut. Antique shops the same. Motels, B&Bs emptied out. The seasonal restaurant owners have left for Boca and Belize. Spring's a long dream away. The lobstermen are mostly come to shore, their traps stacked in their yards, their painted buoys like soldiers mustered into squads. Only here and there a morning café's open, a bar with weekend music. They make it through. The land for a time turns away from the ocean and zips itself up. "It's like Canada here," I heard a child say down on the frigid dock in Belfast, where the fishing boats no longer come, the fishing all fished out. I understood this to mean that the cold just stands up on its own feet here and the big bay stretches forth like tundra, and that the heartbeat of things has slowed.

Yet even though the light drains out of the day by 4 p.m., when there *is* light you can see more now. It *is* some different in winter. Across Linekin Bay the white ghosts of summer villas show up, flush against the shallow bluffs of trees. (In summer all would seem shielded, snugged up, private.) Out on an early morning, you see the rucked bottoms of working boats hauled up dry and nested in cradles beside the summer floats stacked in the corners of the boatyards. A few people are about, but not many. More vivid, more prayerful, is the sudden white spire of the Methodists, the scroll of smoke from an unseen cabin never imagined back there in the woods. "I like the fact that the houses are not lined up along the streets but are scattered around with a kind of independence," a friend writes to me in answer to a picture postcard I've sent to illustrate my surroundings. Yes, I think. You need to spend the winter here. It gets clearer, stripped down, becomes naked in a good way. The allures of summer seem flimsy before these long, slow months of spying on the world through icy windows. In winter you see what's truly supportable, and what's not. Even the sea seems different. The gray smoky light diffuses over the thickened water. Few boats to see. No horizon.

Life ashore. The curling rink's lights are ablaze at 7 p.m. The girls' basketball is on at the gym. Guernseys slowly plod across the oil road toward the frozen, puddled barn lot and the milking parlors. Their dreamy eyes shine yellow in my car lights as I take the back road up to Dry Mill. The dairyman, barely visible behind his dog, pauses in his lot to watch me ease past. "Here in New England, each season carries with it a hundred foreshadowings of the season that is to follow"—E. B. White, himself from away, a New Yorker, wrote this from Allen Cove in 1955—"which is one of the things I love about it. Winter is rough and long, but spring lies all round about." This, in truth, I have failed to notice.

Instead, the wind seems an enemy. The softened thump of cars wearing chains and murmuring past my house late at night, headlights hugging the snowy mat, conspire to leave me edgy, wanton. No hint of spring in these sensations. If only the movie theater were open. My choice would be *Last Tango in Paris*. Someone—a woman I met in Belfast—writes me an unhappy letter: "We love hard, and we hate harder here," she says, in crisp, typed letters below her green monogrammed address, in case I want to take the matter further. "You'd better go where there are other people like you. South of here, mainly." (No pun, I assume, intended.) Of course this startles me, here in my silent, innocent house, though finally less than the absence of cinema.

Early in the season I have saved a man from drowning, or nearly drowning. From inside my room, I heard his voice for a time. (I was not so quick to know a call for help, a voice in need.) When I stepped out onto the porch that overlooked the little anchorage where I was renting, I saw him in the water, his pale face shattered-looking, aggrieved on the water's surface. Somehow he had fallen from his dinghy. I never learned how. Another man and I took the lone powerboat at the dock and fetched him out. I grasped the heavy wool cloth of his coat just at the shoulder stitching, bending over the splintered gunwale. "I'm too heavy," he said, "you'll never do it." "Oh, yes," I said. "I'll do it." And when he was full in the boat and sunk onto the wet timbers, he looked up at me, his face splotched white, his eyes saucers, shuddering all over in the wind. "My God," he said. "It was so cold. You wouldn't believe how cold it was. And I'm a Mainer." I took him at his word. He never really said thank you. Embarrassment proved too strong.

It goes on—the winter. My first. After a week, the light I've watched on Negro Island simply goes out. And though I check on it early and late, it never burns again. I understand little here. In February I go away awhile, and when I come home my house is frozen. Everything. The pipes. The toilets. The sink taps. The machines that need water to work—all quite solid. There's been a misunderstanding about the heating-oil schedule. In the morning, I walk through the house with the plumber, a talkative, philosophical man named Mr. Schuster. Cold sun shoots in all the

windows, bright across the wide pine flooring. It almost seems warm. Out on the ocean, the water is calm and as gray as an old blanket. The cold in the frozen house, for being so still and inveterate, is sterner than the cold outside. "Oh, sure, sure," Mr. Schuster says in jolly spirits, as he tries a tap on the kitchen sink and smiles at me when it fails to give. "We're solid. But don't worry about it." He has big thick amber fingers and wears a regulation red plaid jacket. "It's winter. What can you do? It happens to us all. It'll be fine once it thaws. Replace them pipes and all." He looks at me, not a Mainer, but acceptable for being present now even as a screw-up.

"How long will that be?" I say.

"How long is the winter?" he says, smiling. "Don't we all wish we knew that? We'd be better off all around, then. That's for sure."

Later in the day I close down the house, lock up, arrange for more oil to be brought—albeit too late—and set off for a trip to last until spring.

Coastal snow, Stonington. Fishing is a year-round business. Storms keep fishermen off the water for short periods of time, but it is common to see boats venture out in fog, rain, and snow.

Long Cove, Deer Isle

Lobster shack in snow, Deer Isle

Sunset, Northwest Harbor, Deer Isle. Ice cakes form in coves during extremely cold temperatures. During extended periods of arctic temperatures, entire bays ice over.

114

Sunset reflections, Caterpillar Hill, Sedgwick

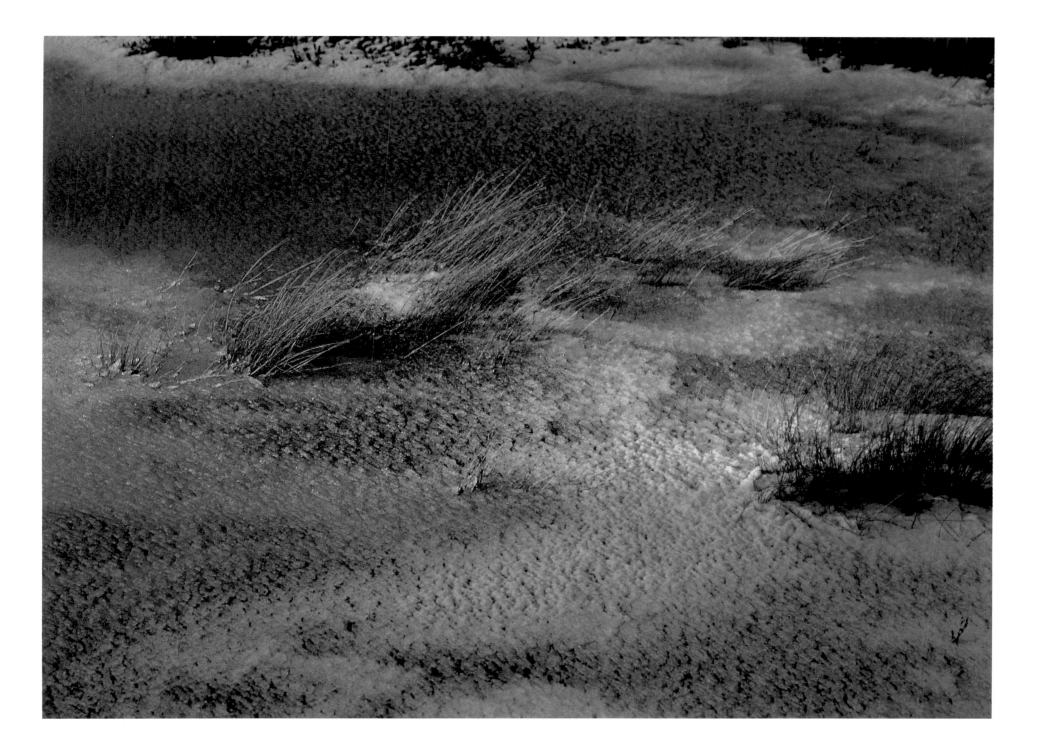

Grass detail at sunset, Sedgwick

Blueberry field in snow, Sedgwick

Blueberry field, Sedgwick. Blueberry bushes hold on to their red color even in the bleakest part of winter. In spring they produce small white blossoms, but the leaves turn crimson again in the fall.

Frozen puddle detail, Deer Isle

Frosted window detail, Deer Isle

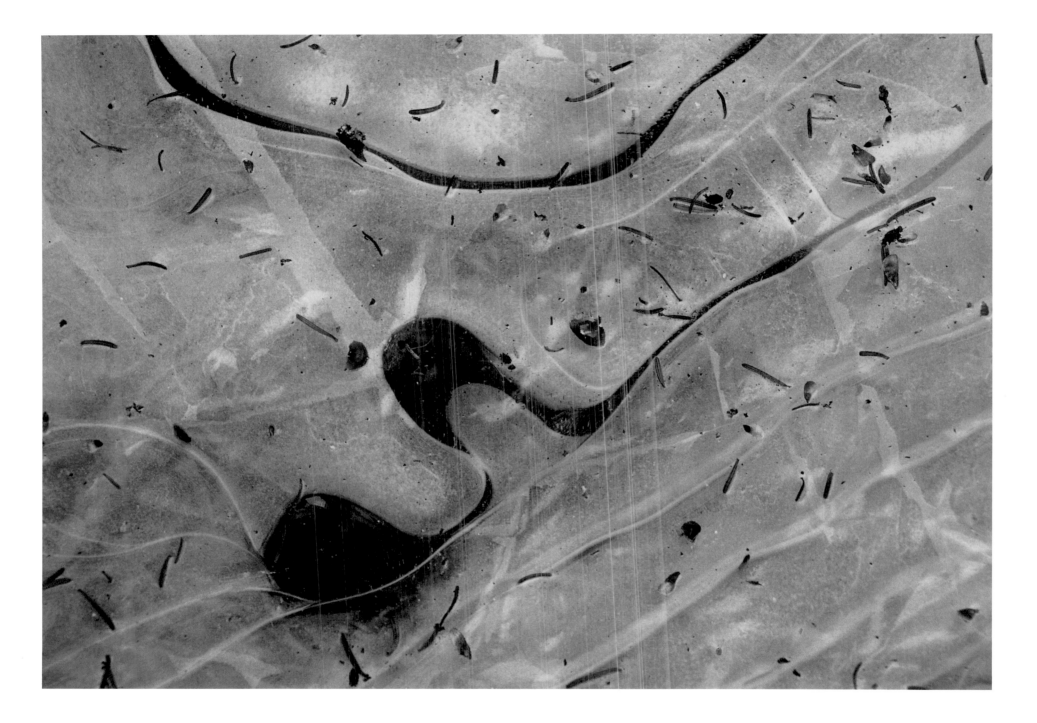

Ice detail, Sedgwick

Opposite: Derelict farmhouse, Sedgwick

Above: Birdhouse in snow, Deer Isle

Dory, Stonington. "If ya ain't busy, it's 'cause ya don't want to be" is the credo of lobstermen who spend their time repairing fishing gear in winter.

Shore houses in snow, Stonington

Lobster boats in ice cakes, Burnt Cove, Deer Isle

Coastal snow, Stonington. Winter weather systems come and go quickly along the coast. There are few prolonged cloudy or sunny days.

Above: Boats in snow, Stonington. Stabilizer sails are used by lobster fishermen to help steady the boats in rolling seas.

Opposite: The Amy-Patty, *sea smoke, Stonington. Many lobster fishermen name their boats with great pride for the wives and daughters who wait each day for their return from the sea.*

Boats at mooring, sea smoke, Stonington. In winter, fishermen drag for shellfish and scuba dive ir frigid waters to harvest sea scallops and urchins by hand.

Twenty below zero, Stonington

Sheep in snow, Stonington

Island sunset, Deer Isle

Below: Frozen sea foam, Deer Isle. It is not uncommon for windchill temperatures in winter to reach minus fifty degrees. At these temperatures, tearing eyes freeze shut, exposed skin is numb, and lungs burn with every breath.

Opposite: Breaking storm, Greenlaw Cove, Deer Isle

Deer Isle Thcrofare. Mainers jokingly say, "There are four seasons here: early winter, midwinter, late winter, and next winter." In January, this seems not far from the truth.

Ocean Drive, Acadia National Park

136

It's as though the forwardness of nature forces in me a piercing and poignant nostalgia. I suddenly remember how the sun falls on granite stones and bakes them warm. How it bathes the moss in the woods bright green. How all sorts of things begin poking up through the pine needles: fiddleheads ready to unfurl, a trillium in bloom, deep green leaves of wild lilies of the valley, white Indian pipes, violets, hepaticas. . . .

On the streets, however, people passing by on their way to the local store may say only a brief "Nice day." After all, at night it still gets cold. This remains sobering. Some mornings you wake to find a thin film of ice covering the water in the birdbath.

It really isn't until Memorial Day that you can be fairly certain the evenings will be warm. You keep the windows open then, even at night, so the world stays with you and there is no longer that sense of being shut away. Now there's a job to do: it's time to fill the window boxes with geraniums and Patient Lucys and petunias, line the walkways with marigolds, begin the battle with the slugs.

Meanwhile, timothy grass grows alongside the back roads, and the fields are budding with tiny bluets, daisies, and buttercups. Lilacs in shades of purple and blue and white are showing their pendant blossoms next to houses, brick libraries, and schools. In the woods, pink lady's slippers bloom and ferns unfurl. Starflowers, low to the ground, stand out vividly against the floor of pine needles. On the spruce trees an inch of soft green new growth shows on the ends of the branches. Honeysuckle climbs along stone walls, and bees zip back and forth in the sun.

By June the world seems as green as green can be. Skinny poplars with their newly opened leaves stand by riverbanks, tender as young schoolgirls. Maple and birch leaves dip and swoop in air so bright that it is hard to remember the world any other way. Blue forget-me-nots have spread through the gardens, and soon the wild rugosa roses will bloom in abundance as they ramble over fences and stone walls. In another few weeks, heavy-handed peonies will lean on white picket fences.

This world on the brink of summer is as beautiful as one could hope to find it. The high sun and wide skies of day bring an openness that lingers through the twilight. Once more there is the smoke from barbecues, the sound of children calling, the scent of mowed grass. Sitting on a porch, looking out over a field or the ocean, you realize the waiting is over. Here is what was whispered of in February. What was promised has arrived.

ELIZABETH STROUT

Spring in Maine begins with a change in the February light.

In February, there will come a morning when I sense some widening of the skies, and sure enough, by afternoon there will be a particular hue of gold to a light so strong that for a few hours it seems to make my heart expand. This light will slap itself up against the sides of brick buildings and wooden houses and old barns. And it will begin to melt the snow. Little rivulets will run alongside the road; the tree trunks will darken from the dripping wet.

But then it will be over—for a while.

The air in February goes from a moist chilliness right back to cold. Evening still comes early. Nighttime is a winter night. Still, once you've felt your heart grow wide, there's no forgetting that quickening of hope, that fleeting sense that something sweet and secretive awaits. And yet the first blossoming snowdrops can be a real surprise. With their tiny green stems and pearly heads bent down, they appear elegant and shy. Little flowers so soon? There they are, though, proof that spring is starting to arrive. The chickadees know it. By the end of February they'll start their mating call. By March the cardinals will be calling, too.

Meanwhile, the days are getting longer, and more and more a softening is taking place, even while the air still has that bite of cold. Every day the sky seems wider as the sun climbs higher and the snow keeps shrinking, dirty at its edges. Around the southern base of tree trunks, you'll find patches of tender green. Then one day, next to the warmth of a house, a yellow crocus will open to the sun. Every year I find this sight amazing: the suddenness of a wide-open flower. Sometimes the first crocus will be purple, but it is always the open yellow crocus that makes me stop and stare.

It might seem that spring in Maine comes on in fits and starts, but something so inexorable is taking place that even a sudden April storm (I can remember one in May) dropping a perfect white snow onto the world isn't going to slow this business down. Because just as suddenly, the sky will become completely blue, and the sun will shine so brilliantly you'll be blinded for a minute by the dazzle—and then will come the shimmer from the quickly melting spring snow, the water dripping steadily off trees. In a few days, there'll be some fat yellow dandelions close to the ground.

As the days get warmer, the air feels sweeter, and in spite of the increasing vim and vigor of color—forsythia bushes that have burst into blossom beside old red barns, daffodils blooming, the tulips that finally open wide—it is this *sweetness* in the air that throws me off guard, causes some restless disturbance in my soul.

Boat in morning fog, Bass Harbor, Mount Desert Island
Previous pages: Lupine field in June, Deer Isle

SPRING

Rugosa roses, Stonington. Blooming rugosas are a sign that visitors "from away" will soon be arriving.

Opposite: Multicolored mosses and lichens, Deer Isle

Right: Lupines in bloom, Deer Isle

Lady's slippers, Deer Isle

Bunchberry blossoms, erratic boulder, Sedgwick

Opposite: Mosses and lichens in maritime fog forest, Crockett Cove, Deer Isle

Right: Wild mushrooms, Deer Isle

Above: White-tailed deer, Deer Isle

Opposite: Crockett Cove, Deer Isle

Thawing ice detail, Deer Isle

Bald eagle, Ames Pond, Stonington

Right: Sunrise, Pickering Cove, Deer Isle. Many islands dot the ocean surrounding Deer Isle, once a hub for sailing ships engaged in international commerce.

Opposite: Sunrise, Cadillac Mountain, Acadia National Park. Pink granite on Cadillac Mountain shows scars from the last ice age. The glacier's weight was so enormous that it sank mountains into the earth's crust, leaving only the peaks exposed—like the Porcupine Islands of Frenchman Bay.

Above: Lobster boat, Eggemoggin Reach, Deer Isle
Opposite: Lifting fog at sunrise, Deer Isle

*Opposite: Sunset through fog,
Heart Island, Deer Isle*

*Right: Granite outcropping
at Otter Cliffs, Shore Drive,
Acadia National Park*

21

Left: Otter Cliffs, Acadia National Park. The urchin and mussel shells in the foreground were left by seagulls, who carry them there to feed atop the cliffs.

Opposite: Freshwater pool, Schoodic Point

Opposite: Traps on wharf, Stoning-
ton. Old ways die hard, but progress
wins. Most traditional wood lobster
traps have been replaced with traps
made of plastic-coated wire.

Right: Dead boat, Corea

Opposite: Lobster traps in "dooryard," Stonington. Mountains of fishing gear are stored on shore during the winter months, when it "blows hard." They are "set out" in late spring after storms "lay down" and "spiders" (lobsters) begin to "crawl" near shore.

Below: Petunias in bloom, Stonington Harbor

A NOTE ON THE TYPE

This book was set in Mrs. Eaves, a typeface designed in 1996 by Zuzanna Licko and modeled after the work of John Baskerville but named for Sarah Eaves, who became Baskerville's wife after the death of her first husband.

Zuzanna Licko (b. 1961) is a type designer with more than thirty typeface families to her credit. She is a cofounder of Emigre, a pioneer digital type foundry.

Composition and color separations by North Market Street Graphics, Lancaster, Pennsylvania

Printing and binding by Tien Wah Press, Singapore

Design by Peter A. Andersen

Window detail, Jericho Bay, Deer Isle

A NOTE ABOUT THE AUTHOR

Terrell S. Lester is a self-taught landscape photographer who first picked up a camera when he was thirty-two years old. In 1987, on his first trip to Maine, he visited Deer Isle, and he has lived there ever since. His work is represented in collections around the world and by more than twenty galleries in the United States.

ACKNOWLEDGMENTS

I would like to extend my sincere gratitude to the following people for helping bring this book to life.

To Sid Albert, for planting the seed; to Paul Bogaards, for his editorial work and vision; and to David Campanaro, Peter Andersen, Roméo Enriquez, Andy Hughes, Archie Ferguson, Debra Helfand, and all the fine people at Knopf involved in the book's production. A special thank-you to Elizabeth Strout, Ann Beattie, Richard Russo, and Richard Ford for their fabulous essays.

To Cherie and Ken Mason, Ken and Marnie Crowell, Gerry and Sherrel Heanssler, Suzanne and Don Carmichael, Susan and Gardner Smith, Christopher Knight and Katherine Lasky Knight, Nancy Hodermarksy, and Andrew Lund, for their insights, expertise, and thoughtful suggestions.

To family and friends: John and Doris Leiva, Amy Lester, Johnny and Hillary Pearson, H. August and Sally Kuehl, Deborah Schinzing, Garry Lester, Pam Parris, Rhonda Viveney, Andrew Kuehl and Linda Kuehl, Bob and Judy Tredwell, Mary Offutt, Dean and Sandy Chase, Jerry and Betty Downs, Parker Waite, Brenda Gilchrist, Dick and Amelia McKenney, Darwin and Jackie Davidson, Elena Houlihan, and Teresa Ollila.

To all the people of Deer Isle, and to Ken and Jane Black, who pointed the way there.

To my wife, Ginger, whose spirit dwells in every image.

And with a special appreciation for those who work tirelessly to save, maintain, and restore the beauty of the natural world.

My gratitude to all.

Nights and days came and passed

And summer and winter

and the sun and the wind

and the rain.

And it was good to be a little Island.

A part of the world

and a world of its own

all surrounded by the bright blue sea.

—GOLDEN MACDONALD

(MARGARET WISE BROWN),

The Little Island

SUMMER

Dory at sunrise, Stonington

ANN BEATTIE

Summer in Maine, like any other season in Maine, is filled with contradictions. The flowers are plentiful, but it seems that many people choose to plant annuals instead of perennials, then spend the summer fretting (or are they perversely happy?) that they'll have to plant their beautiful flowers all over again next year. If you live in Maine, you come to terms with long stretches of cold, dark days that gradually prickle with sunlit spots and soothe with some not-so-frigid breezes. Everyone looks forward to the joyous arrival of spring, which quickly leads into summer—always-too-short summer. Summer is the time to repaint, to replant, to enact a kind of charade of easy life, because soon enough the days will shorten, the light will change, the birds will migrate, and the cat won't be so eager to leave the house. Summer in Maine is postcard-beautiful: enjoyable, inspiring, demanding. Demanding because there is always the knowledge that summer days are few, and that what you do or don't accomplish will bring you a sense of pride or a feeling of frustration come fall.

When people think of Maine, they often conjure up the rocky coast, the lighthouses, the sailboats on fantastically blue water. Of course the beaches are crowded by day, with mothers gathering up beach toys and smearing suntan lotion on their children's pale skin. But nighttime at the shore can be even more fun. That's when dogs and their Frisbee-throwing friends are allowed. That's when the mothers have become less-frantic wives (the children having been tucked in bed by baby-sitters), strolling hand-in-hand with their husbands at twilight. The idea of romance, I think, is not the first thing people associate with Maine. With Venice, perhaps. Or Paris. But Maine? Feisty, frugal Maine, with that frigid water and those rather fearsome seagulls? I'm not much of a romantic, but part of the reason I'm seduced by the state is the fact that you have to search a little, you have to stay awhile, to discover the romance. It isn't apparent on the surface. Sure, any place with moonlight on the water is romantic; but there's a certain mystery to the way Maine metamorphoses from a daytime playground to a quieter, more enigmatic, more spacious place at night.

When I was a child, my parents would drive from Washington, D.C., to Maine most summers to enjoy the three-mile-long beach in Ogunquit, and to see summer theater and take walks along the sand. Like many people, they also went for the crispy fried clams and the cool night breezes. I remember that we always remembered the previous vacation wrong and therefore never had enough sweaters, and that the greenhead flies on the beach at dusk sent us running. Maine seemed exotic; it might as well have been another country, it was so different from where I grew up. I don't think it ever occurred to me that setting lobster traps and hauling them up was hard work—I just thought of lobster as my dinner. The July days I spent in Maine were easy, sunny, and breezy, and the nights were refreshingly cool. Summer seemed to be there for the taking, and most of the people who lived there year-round were dependent enough on the tourist trade to be polite; if waiters and innkeepers were not exactly effusive, well, that was the stereotype of the New Englander. It never occurred to me that the services they provided were bracketed in their minds by difficult winters. I didn't think about that, about what it must be like when the snows came, followed by snowplows. The easy summer is for vacationers, not year-rounders, who annually have to endure a bizarre sort of Christmas in July, with tourists like hyperventilating elves busily having fun and preparing presents for no one but themselves. At the end of the day, so very many lobsters sent out on steaming trays to hungry diners must make you think that Santa has gone a little strange and come up with the same gift idea over and over again.

It's not all that fanciful to associate Christmas with summer in Maine. There are more Christmas shops than you might expect, catering to the tourist trade. What is the assumption? That winter is coming faster than you think—so you need to be reminded? As well as a way to make money, aren't those shops a little elbow in the ribs? The decorations look so incongruous on a sunny, salty day: the icicles and glittering reindeer; the miniature Christ child in the crèche. What you see around you are intensely colored flowers and, outside the tourist centers (or at least I hope so), sleek foxes and plump rabbits; the Snuglee strapped to Mom's or Dad's chest and containing a slumbering baby is the modern-day manger.

· · ·

I live in Maine now half the year. I'm there not so much because of fond childhood memories as because my husband likes to sail, and he has something of a history in the state (though it isn't counted in triple digits, so I realize it doesn't count). I'm a snowbird: I run away when it looks like things might get serious. Serious means: gray days; early (if spectacular) sunsets; cold. Those times I've lingered into winter, I've been stunned that summer seems farther behind than chronological time tells me it is. It's as if grayness erases your memory of all that summer color; it's as if the days fold in on themselves, instead of expanding the way a great summer day expands.

But again, it's Maine's contradictions that make it so interesting, at least for a writer. When you take in the view, your eye always moves between the general and the particular, the faraway and the up-close: the huge stretch of the Atlantic Ocean and the tiny snail on the rocks; the large expanse of marshland and the mosquito on the tip of your nose. There can be the seductive suggestion that things are endlessly plentiful: the wild blueberries; the sunny days; the perfect photo-ops; the seemingly constant supply of fresh fish. But it isn't so: there's poison ivy growing amid the blueberries; the rain and fog will come; the sun will disappear behind a cloud just when you've found your perfect photograph; there's been too much overfishing. Sadly, there are not so many mussels as there used to be. Or scallops. Or most anything else. The truth is, Maine is a serious place masquerading as a summer paradise. A place where the price of land has driven fishermen farther from the water. Where, in a booming economy, hotels and restaurants have to import workers—often from countries far from New England. And, increasingly, a place where people camp out only for the so-called good months. Workers in my town live

*Dories and lobster boat, Stonington. Dories, once used to locate herring, have been
replaced by spotter planes and satellite navigation.*

in group houses; everything turns on the dollar. Time-share condominiums allow everybody a moment in the very, very upscale tent.

Of course, you can also camp in the woods. The woods are . . . woods. They're the paradoxical woods of Robert Frost's famous poem, woods that are at once "lovely, dark and deep." Nature in Maine is your friend or your enemy. It depends on how you view it. And also on your luck.

. . .

Summer is my favorite time of the year in Maine. Not just because it's Not Winter, but because the season is wonderful in its own right: that's what all those cars are doing on the highway. That's why the farmer's market is as crowded as Harrods' food court. Everybody loves the same season I love; they want to be hiking Mount Katahdin and sailing on Penobscot Bay and eating wild blueberries. The clichés are really quite pleasant: the gulls that are said to swoop (no mention of the racket they make, drowning out any attempt at conversation); the boats touchingly named for men's true loves, such as the *Lovely Lucinda* (as opposed to the boats bobbing in the water that commemorate men's other love, money—like the *Puts and Calls*).

Maine takes a lot of kidding: the reputedly taciturn people, ever the butt of jokes; the blackflies, exaggerated into single-engine planes by stand-up comedians; the water that curls your toes. What do all those daytrippers want to see? They often don't make it to the farther reaches of the state, where the wind on Isle au Haut can make your ears ache so much you wish you'd brought earmuffs, and where the cliffs seem to either magnetize you to the edge or propel you back instantly, depending on your testosterone level and/or your personality. Who are they, all those people—more and more every year—who come expecting sweet corn and sweet dreams? To them, Maine is the paintings of Fairfield Porter and the Wyeths; it is the poem they memorized, though they might not quite have understood it. What to say of a place that—according to *Fodor's 2000*—is so large that all the other states of New England could fit within its perimeters?

That it offers the possibility of space. Peace. Tranquillity. That it is a sort of vanished America that nevertheless exists, partly in a time warp, partly as part of the modern age. The adventurous can have their adventures—rock climbing, kayaking, deer hunting. The timid can be catered to at imposing hotels, where there are flowery cushions on wicker rocking chairs. Some of these chairs will face the water, and over the water will appear lovely sunsets and a glowing moon. Those things might be present the rest of the year wherever the tourist lives, but in Maine the spectacle is something one stops for. Summer in Maine can easily be described through synesthesia: the dawn tastes delicious; the distant mountain hums. And much of the hard work that keeps it going—that keeps New York City going, for that matter—happens behind the scenes, under cover of darkness, from the deck of a lobster boat in the predawn, from behind the wheel of a long-distance truck transporting Maine's products. There is so much, you will never know it all. It is a world that is beautiful, colorful, drenched in an indescribable light: a world that could easily be unreal, except it is not. Maine is just far away—in both distance and spirit—from other places. It is a place we stop imagining to look, and look to imagine.

Opposite: Dock in fog, Stonington. The lobster crates in the foregound are used for holding lobsters in underwater holding pens called cars.

Above: Lobster traps and lobster pot with flowers, Stonington. Islands are, by necessity, places of strong community. One of the many ways people participate is by decorating a public place.

Derelict cars in saltwater farm pasture, Stonington

Wild azaleas, Mount Katahdin, Baxter State Park

40

Shadbush blossoms,
Walker Pond,
Sedgwick

Sandy Stream Pond, Baxter State Park

Slide dam, Baxter State Park

Big Eddy, Golden Road, North Woods

Above: Sunrise, Cupsuptic Lake

Opposite: Sunrise, Elbow Pond, Mount Katahdin, Baxter State Park

Introduced decades ago as ornamental plants, water-lilies have become a local attraction at Ames Pond near Stonington.

Dories and lobster shack, Stonington

Lobster boat, Stave Island, Deer Isle

The Penny Pincher, *Stonington. Fishermen step from kitchen table to boat, much as many of us jump into cars for the morning commute.*

Buoy markers at sunrise, Stonington. The colors of the buoy markers identify a fisherman's gear. Fishing areas are territorial, and disputes have led to infamous "lobster wars."

Storm wave, Schoodic Peninsula. Unimpeded by islands, storm waves from the Gulf of Maine crash head–on into sheer granite cliffs at Schoodic Point.

Bass Harbor Head Light, Mount Desert Island. Since 1858, Bass Harbor Head Light has provided a beacon for navigation along the treacherous coast.

Otter Cliffs, Acadia National Park

Sunrise, Otter Cliffs,
Acadia National Park

Above: Dories in yard, Monhegan Island

Opposite: Harbor sunset, Monhegan Island. Year-round living on Monhegan Island represents isolation to some, but most residents relish the quiet lifestyle far from the mainland

Tidal cove, Corea

Rockweed at low tide,
Blue Hill Falls

Left: Tree stump at low tide,
Heart Island, Deer Isle

Opposite: Incoming tide,
Heart Island, Deer Isle

AUTUMN

RICHARD RUSSO

Though he never set foot in the state, my grandfather would have been a natural Mainer. When I was a boy, he was already in the autumn of his life, having survived two world wars, the Depression, and a daily existence too full of Duty (both secular and religious). Prematurely bald and rail thin from the malaria he'd contracted in the Philippines, he concluded that he would not live to be an old man. Or, more precisely, he believed that sixty *was* old. When he spoke of dying, as if it were something he meant to do next week, or the week after, as soon as things slowed down and he could get around to it, the idea filled me with terror, because I loved him and couldn't imagine the world without him, and the thought that a man could contemplate his own mortality with such perfect equanimity seemed perverse to a boy my age. Worse, my grandfather's reasoning was impossible to follow. On the one hand, he seemed to believe that what life called for was constant vigilance. If you didn't pay attention and plan ahead, when the winter came you'd run out of coal and freeze, or you'd run out of food and starve, or run out of money and have to go naked. On the other hand, he cheerfully conceded that something along these lines might just happen anyway, whether you paid attention or not, because Winter always had

a few tricks up its sleeve that you'd be lucky to anticipate. As I say, he'd have made a great Mainer.

In Maine, at least midcoast, where I live, the first leaves start to turn in mid-August. This is a sobering sight, one that calls to mind the white, hooded figure in N. C. Wyeth's *A Winter*. He's already stalking us, and probably has been all summer long. In Maine, winter is reality, summer a lovely illusion, and those first August-orange leaves are a reminder of this hard truth. After Labor Day, all's fair, but when the temperature's in the eighties and the days are still long enough for my wife and me to take our walks after dinner instead of before, this notice is hard to swallow. Just as sixty is too soon to be resigned to death, the third week in August is too soon to be reminded of approaching winter, especially with some of Maine's finer pleasures on our doorstep.

Come September, the tourists that have clogged the streets of every village from Kittery to Bar Harbor will head home, taking with them their car alarms and cell phones and digital cameras and hi-tech baby strollers and hip-hop CDs. The sleek sailing vessels will tack away, their propellers snagging lobster pots in their hasty departure, returning our harbors to the lumbering, boxy fishing boats and the men who work the water year-round. After Labor

Young hardwoods on Golden Road, near Baxter State Park. Colors are bright on overcast days along Golden Road, which was named by locals for the cost of construction, not the fall colors.

Day we can walk into any restaurant on the coast without a reservation. The price of lobster drops and tiny rural farm stands groan under the weight of real tomatoes and corn. Nearby you'll find a battered scale for weighing what you've put into secondhand supermarket bags, and also a wooden box containing coins and dollar bills from which it is expected that you will make honest change. And yet such seeming Keatsian abundance is also largely an illusion. Yes, the gourd doth swell in Maine and the trees do bend with apples under the maturing sun, but Maine's rocky soil will never feed the world. The tomatoes will disappear with the first frost, the one right around the corner, leaving only a few killer zucchini, good mostly for jokes and compost. No, in Maine you won't find Autumn sitting careless on the granary floor, her hair soft-lifted by the winnowing wind, drowsed by the fume of poppies. By mid-September the wind off the Atlantic is both earnest and portentous, making Mainers more watchful than drowsy. Did we put in enough wood? Did we ever complete the form sent to us by our heating oil company back in June, locking in the price? How long does antifreeze retain its potency? we wonder, knowing we can't afford to be wrong. Winter is coming and not even the proximity of L.L. Bean, with its bumper crop of Gortex and Thinsulate and fleece and scratchy wool, is all that reassuring.

Autumn, as my grandfather understood, is the season of paradox. When the leaves turn, when the physical world is at its most heartbreakingly beautiful, what we are witnessing, purely and simply, is death. In the autumn of his life, my grandfather loved the fall, loved the smell of burning leaves. He took as perfectly natural the fact that wood smoke penetrated his emphysema-diminished lungs more deeply and satisfyingly than even the pure oxygen from the tank that stood at attention behind his green armchair, the chair where, after a life of worrying that he'd run out of fuel or food or money, he would run out of air.

I, like my grandfather, am both a worrier and a lover of autumn. It is the time of year, at least in Maine, when those of us inclined to worry find our inclinations most validated by nature. (One is a fool to worry in summer; by winter it's too late.) Each October for the last several years, my daughters and I have climbed nearby Mount Megunticook, which overlooks the ragged midcoast. From the cliffs at the top, the village where we live sits almost directly below. If the sun is bright and the sky cloudless—and such a day will always be available in mid-October—the reflection of light off the ocean can be almost painful, its shimmer musically surreal. Toss in a couple of schooners under full sail, just barely identifiable for what they are from such a height, a vast carpet of peak foliage extending as far as the eye can see, and a plain white church steeple or two, and a middle-aged man with two smart, beautiful college-bound daughters just might—despite his hereditary inclinations—find himself guilty of optimism. On such an afternoon, lying back on the warm rocks, my sweat from the climb drying in the crisp air, I could almost be convinced that nature just might reverse itself this year and head back in the other direction toward summer, of which we Mainers never quite get our fill. Almost.

But of course the late-afternoon trek down the mountain is darker, the leaves underfoot not so much beautiful as wet and treacherous. Somewhere along the path the air turns from cool and crisp to chill and clammy, and in that moment something pivots on its fulcrum and it occurs to a man like my grandfather— and, yes, a man like me—that now would be a good time to make a

Bear River, near Grafton Notch State Park. A blanket of deciduous hardwood leaves camouflages the river.

Foliage, Lily Bay State Park,
Moosehead Lake

show of competence: to service the furnace, to make sure the chimney flue hasn't rusted shut, to check that the gutters are not clogged with leaves. Time to find the lamps and the bottles of clear oil we'll need when the ice storm comes and we're again without electricity. And batteries.

By the time we reach the bottom of the trail and emerge from the woods into the flat, empty campground. I've made a mental list. It's a partial one at best, and like my grandfather I'm smart enough to know that what I'll end up needing most probably isn't on it, but by worrying, I've already fulfilled my first autumnal duty. Worry is not competence, but we make do with the former since the latter may reside only in our imaginations—or in summer, when it's not really needed.

72

Screw Auger Falls,
Grafton Notch State Park

Frosted swamp at sunrise, Sedgwick

Blueberry field in fog, Sedgwick

Blueberry bushes and birch trees, Caterpillar Hill, Sedgwick

Above: Decoys in lobster shack, Deer Isle. Traditional craft and ingenuity mix in Downeast fishing communities. Skills like boat-building and woodworking are used for recreation as well as survival.

Opposite: Storm light, Stonington. The first storms of winter come in late October. Some fishermen will put their gear on shore for the winter, while others will set their gear in deeper water.

Moonset, Cadillac Mountain, Acadia National Park. The light of sunrise first touches the continental United States on top of Cadillac Mountain, drawing many visitors to the summit daily.

Caterpillar Hill, Sedgwick. Surrounded by white pine needles and crimson blueberry leaves, an erratic glacial boulder lies where it was deposited at the end of the last ice age.

Autumn color detail, Acadia National Park

Maple leaves, Big Eddy, West Branch, Penobscot River. The West Branch of the Penobscot River was once used to drive timber to mills. Now it is a favorite spot of sport fishermen and white-water boating enthusiasts.

Below: Caterpillar Hill, overlooking Deer Isle/Stonington Bridge and Little Deer Isle

Opposite: Caterpillar Hill, Sedgwick. In autumn, crimson blueberry fields blanket rolling hills overlooking Penobscot Bay and the Camden Hills.

Opposite: Approaching storm, Frenchman Bay, Acadia mountains

Above: Autumn sunrise, Stave Island, Deer Isle

Left: Harvest moon, Stonington

*Opposite: Moose Island Point, Stoning-
ton. Rounded by natural elements, pink
granite boulders are found throughout
eastern Penobscot Bay and the Mount
Desert Island area.*

88

Blueberry barren, Caterpillar Hill, Sedgwick. Blueberry barrens have a boreal appearance, with the look and feel of arctic tundra. Not long ago, moose and caribou foraged in these fields.

White birch trees in fall colors, Baxter State Park. The northern terminus of the Appalachian Trail is Mount Katahdin in Baxter State Park.

Bear River, Grafton Notch State Park

Trees felled by beavers, Schooner Head Road, Acadia National Park

Lower South Branch Pond, Baxter State Park. A gift of Governor Percival Baxter to the people of Maine in 1931, Baxter State Park now encompasses some 200,000 acres of wilderness.

Ripogenus Lake, North Woods. Tree stumps are symbols of clear-cut logging methods that are no longer practical.

Opposite: Abol Pond, Baxter State Park. Winter in Maine's North Woods does not arrive subtly. In a few days, Abol Pond will be frozen solid.

Above: Ice film on Mink Pond, Baxter State Park. Bogs and ponds abound along Rum Brook in Baxter State Park.

Above: Near Rum Brook, Baxter State Park

Opposite: Helon Taylor Pond, Baxter State Park. The rugged summit of Mount Katahdin is nearly a mile high and presents a strenuous challenge to the hundreds who make the ascent each year.

Big Eddy, West Branch, Penobscot River

Togue Pond,
Baxter State Park

Bull moose, Sandy Stream Pond, Baxter State Park

Sandy Stream Pond, Baxter State Park

Autumn snowfall, Mount Katahdin, Baxter State Park

Moonrise, Stave Island, Deer Isle

Sunrise, Mill Pond, Deer Isle

WINTER